Living Lenten Portraits

LIVING LENTEN PORTRAITS

Nine Dramatic Monologs

Richard Andersen

Publishing House
St. Louis　London

Scripture quotations so identified are from *The Living Bible Paraphrased,* copyright © 1971 by Tyndale House Publishers, Wheaton, Ill. 60187. Used by permission of Tyndale House Publishers.

Scripture quotations so identified are from *The New English Bible.* © The Delegates of the Oxford University Press and The Syndics of the Cambridge University Press 1961, 1970. Reprinted by permission.

Scripture quotations so identified are from the *Today's English Version of the New Testament.* Copyright © American Bible Society 1966, 1971.

Scripture quotations so identified are from the *Revised Standard Version* of the Bible, copyright 1946 and 1952 by the Division of Christian Education, National Council of Churches, and used by permission.

Concordia Publishing House, St. Louis, Missouri
Concordia Publishing House Ltd., London, E. C. 1
Copyright © 1975 Concordia Publishing House

MANUFACTURED IN THE UNITED STATES OF AMERICA

Library of Congress Cataloging in Publication Data
Andersen, Richard, 1931-
    Living Lenten portraits.
    1. Monologues. 2. Bible—Biography. I. Title. PN4231.A5
812'.5'4   74-16294   ISBN 0-570-03196-6

SOLI DEO GLORIA

For those who are experimenting with me
in a thrilling new challenge in the development
of the Community Church of Joy,
Glendale, Arizona

Contents

Introduction	9
Isaiah	13
Bartimaeus	23
John the Baptist	31
Matthew	37
Caiaphas	45
Paul	51
Judas	59
Pilate	67
Cleopas	74

Introduction

In recent years the Christian church has witnessed a revival of various art forms in the worship services. Morality and passion plays have dramatized Scriptural events and themes for centuries. The use of monolog and dialog sermons, playlets, and a variety of musical forms, as well as films and filmstrips and multimedia presentations are to be encountered in many churches today. Pastors and parishioners have voiced their delight over the imaginative use of these forms in traditional worship settings. This collection of *Living Lenten Portraits* aims at adding to the wealth of material currently available.

These brief sermonic monologs are simple to stage, costume, and perform. They are not intended to be avant garde portrayals, but characterizations that young and old can enjoy, find inspiring, and glean some factual background material from to stimulate their thoughts in the direction of Easter. Hopefully the portrayals will stimulate pastors and parishioners to develop their own characterizations also. Armed with several good Bible translations, a Bible dictionary, and a few other helpful resource books, the average person can bring to the 20th century any Biblical character he desires.

I found these guidelines helpful in developing the Lenten service in parishes I have served. They are not intended to be restrictive.

1. Strive for brevity and fill the time with inspiration! There is no reason why a midweek service needs to be long to be meaningful. Aim at half-hour services scheduled early enough in the evening so that whole families may attend.
2. Be innovative. If a liturgical form is required, employ one of the suffrages in *The Lutheran Hymnal* or the *Service Book and Hymnal,* adapt one of the forms provided in the *Worship Supplement,* or build the monolog into a service of the Word produced by the Inter-Lutheran Commission on Worship. A simple service may include invocation, several appropriate hymns (a good time to introduce some contemporary songs that fit the season and theme of the evening), special music, significant Bible readings (read from the congregation by laymen, read in unison from Scripture portions, etc.), and pertinent prayers.
3. Involve the laity. Invite their participation in both the portrayals and conducting the liturgy. Vest the liturgists and rehearse the service together so they may have the benefit of pastoral guidance before they take to the chancel. It's a good time to put the deacons and elders to work. One person can do all the portrayals, or several can participate.
4. Glorifying God and inspiring His people are your foremost goals. Don't get fussy about making authentic costumes or building the-way-it-was-in-Bible-times sets. Let the people use their imaginations. I have prepared a brief description of costumes and equipment needed for each portrayal. Use your own imagination in improvising the furnishings suggested. Wear modern street

clothes if you prefer. Costuming is not required.
5. Rehearse the characterization often. Get into the role. Practice in costume. Work at becoming the character. If it requires a change of voice, a peculiar form of walk, etc., don't be so stuffy that you can't let the character shine through your own personality. Bend! Be flexible! Don't worry over memorization. Use lecterns or place the portions of the script near the spots where you'll be standing. Know the script well enough so that you are not totally dependent on it. If anything is to be memorized, it's the "bridges" that get you from one place to the other. The important idea is to develop the character. Work on that instead of memorization.

As far as costumes are concerned, few congregations can afford to rent authentic outfits or make costumes that are absolutely authentic. Thrift, imagination, and resourcefulness are your best assets in preparing a wardrobe that suggests the character being portrayed. Remnant materials in coarse weaves and bright colors, including stripes, are inexpensive and serve well. Look for sales. Buy second-rate materials at discount houses! Long tunics and short cloaks, or long cloaks and short tunics with contrasting sashes and headgear can be worn interchangeably to provide several different costumes. Leather sandals or bare feet serve as standard footwear. Hemmed yardage can be draped on furniture or worn. Cheap jewelry for some characters adds to the costuming. If you lack inspiration, examine Sunday school leaflets and Bible story books for suggestions. Remember to aim at simplicity, however.

Quotations in this collection are from several Bible translations, including the Revised Standard Version, J. B. Phillips, The Living Bible, King James, and The New English Bible.

May these *Living Lenten Portraits* serve you and the Lord well.

RICHARD ANDERSEN

ISAIAH

Isaiah is dressed in the traditional tunic and cloak with sandals and headgear made of a piece of cloth fitted to the head by a woman's braided hairband.

The prophet uses two scrolls during the portrayal, which are placed on the steps of the chancel beforehand. A lectern is in the center aisle at the chancel steps. The scrolls are made out of brown paper, fastened to two dowels (half-inch diameter) with wooden drawer pulls on each end. Use narrow velvet ribbon to tie each scroll, and be sure to mark them so you will know which scroll is to be read first.

Type the passages you desire to read on a sheet of paper and affix to the scrolls. Some passages are suggested, but you may wish to use others. Select passages from Isaiah concerning Christ's nativity for the first scroll, and passages concerning His sacrifice for the second one. Use whatever translations most satisfactorily explain themselves to a contemporary congregation of mixed ages.

Clue the choir (or a group of worshipers seated in various places in the congregation) to respond to the salutation: "The Lord be with you." Their response is "And with thy spirit."

This portrayal may be adapted to either Advent or Lenten worship.

To add something different from the other portrayals, have the prophet enter from a different way than other characters have come into the chancel.

Isaiah

ISAIAH 1:1; LUKE 4:16-21

(Hands outstretched in greeting) The Lord be with you!
(Choir responds) And with thy spirit!

You undoubtedly expected someone a bit different! After all, a prophet is one that many people today consider somewhat weird, but we're really not so different from you. We have the same needs as you do. But God has called us to a special work. At times we foretell what is yet to happen. Most of the time, however, we're preachers concerned with getting God's word out, calling people to faith, and encouraging them in living God-pleasing lives.

That's not so weird, is it?

Your pastors are the prophets of this age. In fact, each believer in the Christ is one of His ministers. But are you ministering?

Are you touching lives with the message of hope?

Are you gathering souls whose experience of God's love enables them to stand above the foolishness of these days?

Are you calling sinners to holiness?

Some have called me a poet, and that I was. Who could walk with God without being touched by the marvel of His concern? I preached and proclaimed, I prodded and persevered. Often I was inspired to eloquence. The book that bears my name in the Old Testament is a collection of many of my sermons, messages that still evoke hope today, that still prod men to righteous living.

I am the son of Amoz, but please don't confuse him with the prophet Amos. My home was in the holy city of Jerusalem, where I was born in the decade of 760 B. C. What a glorious city was Jerusalem. There was God's temple, where I often went to worship and meditate.

I was married to a lovely, faithful girl that many called the "prophetess." I suppose you would consider me weird because I named my sons unusual names, names which symbolized the prophecy I was intent upon preaching.

One son I called "Shear-Jashub," which means "A Remnant Shall Return." How would you like to have such a name as that? And even worse, according to the standards of your day, is "Mahershalalhashbaz," that is "Haste Ye, Speed Ye to the Spoil." They were not pretty names, but they helped people to understand the message I preached.

I lived after the kingdoms of Saul, David, and Solomon had been divided. Israel was to the north, vulnerable to attack, and alien to temple worship in Jerusalem. Amos and Hosea were prophesying there, and they influenced my concern about social conditions in Judah, the southern kingdom, in which I lived and worked. Often my messages began with the attention-getting word "behold!" In that way I was able to focus on issues and troubles and direct people to answers that God provided.

I had the respect of the people. Kings even sought my counsel. You recall the names of Uzziah, Jotham, Ahaz, and Hezekiah certainly. Statesmen and officials came to me for guidance, and in many ways God used me to formulate national policies. There was no separation of church and state, as you call it. My disciples and I were preeminently concerned with preaching God's Word, but in very practical ways, for we intended to influence the ethical, social, and spiritual qualities of life. To many, my message was the voice of God to the people.

Maybe you have heard the ancient legend of my death that says I was placed in a hollow tree and sawn asunder by King Manasseh, but the time and facts of my death are not important, except to scholars. It was not my life I came to promote, but to drum into all the people of Judah the expectation and hopefulness there is in our great God. For that reason you will find joy even in the passages of sorrow in my book, faith in the time of disaster, strength in the time of defeat, and hope when all looks bleak. God's care of His people is tender. Their sins hurt His love, yet He loves His people greatly.

I'm no fly-by-night sentimentalist preaching a shallow kind of happiness, but in my words you will discover anew the greatness of God and the solid joy that is in the Lord despite personal and national heartaches. In Him whatever trouble is encountered is overcome.

When I went about preaching, Judah and Israel both were subject to the might of the powerful neighbors around us. Assyria to the northeast and Egypt to the south threatened the security of my homeland year after year.

Let me illustrate: Little Judah was a pawn between Egypt and Assyria. I wanted to depend on neither for defense against the other, but King Hezekiah allied himself with Egypt. Like a captive I walked through the streets of Jerusalem without my upper garment and shoes on to dramatize the warning the king hesitated to accept. When the Assyrians besieged Jerusalem, Hezekiah was in panic. I spoke to him with firmness, and Jerusalem was spared. I said,

> He shall not enter this city
> nor shoot an arrow there,
> he shall not advance against it with shield
> nor cast up a siege-ramp against it!
> By the way on which he came he shall go back;
> this city he shall not enter.
> This is the very word of the Lord.
> I will shield this city to deliver it,
> for My own sake and for the sake of My servant David.

The Lord did not disappoint us. Jerusalem did not fall! Sennacherib was compelled to withdraw to Mesopotamia because of disturbances at home and the outbreak of plague among his soldiers. But he also tasted the might of God:

"That night the angel of the Lord went out and struck down a hundred and eighty-five thousand men in the Assyrian camp; when morning dawned, they all lay dead." Jerusalem was again safe, a miracle of our wondrous God.

With all the political and military unrest in my day, one might expect me to be a man discouraged and ready to give up or give in, but with such a God as this I could always look hopefully toward the future. Why not? The Messiah was to come! Let me read you the prophecy of the Christ:

(Read from Scroll 1)

"Listen, house of David. Are you not content to wear out men's patience? Must you also wear out the patience of my God? Therefore the Lord himself shall give you a sign: A young woman is with child, and she will bear a son, and will call Him Immanuel."

The people who walked in darkness
have seen a great light:
light has dawned upon them,
   dwellers in a land as dark as death.
Thou hast increased their joy and given them great gladness;
they rejoice in thy presence as men rejoice at harvest,
or as they are glad when they share out the spoil;
   for thou hast shattered the yoke that burdened them,
     the collar that lay heavy on their shoulders,
   the driver's goad, as on the day of Midian's defeat.
   All the boots of trampling soldiers
   and the garments fouled with blood
shall become a burning mass, fuel for fire.
For a boy has been born for us, a son given to us
   to bear the symbol of dominion on his shoulder;
   and he shall be called
   in purpose wonderful, in battle God-like,
   Father for all time, Prince of peace.
Great shall the dominion be,
   and boundless the peace
bestowed on David's throne and on his kingdom
to establish and sustain it
   with justice and righteousness
   from now and for evermore.
The zeal of the Lord of Hosts shall do this.

There's always hope to be found in the Lord God, just as Christians during this Lenten season sense all the more the fulfillment of my prophecies. Beyond Good Friday there is Easter. That's as God would have it, for beyond sin there is forgiveness. Beyond death there is life. Beyond today is tomorrow. Beyond Isaiah there is Christ.

(Read from Scroll 2)

He grew up before the Lord like a young plant
  whose roots are in parched ground;
he had no beauty, no majesty to draw our eyes,
    no grace to make us delight in him;
his form, disfigured, lost all the likeness of a man,
  his beauty changed beyond human semblance.
He was despised, he shrank from the sight of men,
  tormented and humbled by suffering;
  we despised him, we held him of no account,
  a thing from which men turn away their eyes.
Yet on himself he bore our sufferings,
    our torments he endured,
  while we counted him smitten by God,
    struck down by disease and misery;
  but he was pierced for our transgressions,
    tortured for our iniquities;
  the chastisement he bore is health for us
    and by his scourging we are healed.
  We all strayed like sheep,
  each of us had gone his own way;
  but the Lord laid upon him
    the guilt of us all.
  He was afflicted, he submitted to be struck down
    and did not open his mouth;
  he was led like a sheep to the slaughter,
  like a ewe that is dumb before the shearers.
Without protection, without justice, he was taken away;
  and who gave a thought to his fate,
    how he was cut off from the world of living men,
  stricken to the death for my people's transgession?
  He was assigned a grave with the wicked,
  a burial-place among the refuse of mankind,
  though he had done no violence
    and spoken no word of treachery.

> Yet the Lord took thought of his tortured servant
> and healed him who had made himself a sacrifice for sin;
> so shall he enjoy long life and see his children's children,
> and in his hand the Lord's cause shall prosper.
> After all his pains he shall be bathed in light,
> after his disgrace he shall be fully vindicated;
> so shall he, my servant, vindicate many,
> himself bearing the penalty of their guilt.
> Therefore I will allot him a portion with the great,
> and he shall share the spoil with the mighty,
> because he exposed himself to face death
> and was reckoned among transgressors,
> because he bore the sin of many
> and interceded for their transgressions.

As God's prophet, I proclaimed the Suffering Servant that is the Messiah. I exclaimed "Behold!" and the world beheld the glory of God. It's a message that men today need listen to with greater expectancy. If you live in expectancy, trusting God, seeing joy arise out of heartache . . . if you live in expectation of fulfillment, you see not only the prophets' preaching come true in you, but you will see the Messiah in Jesus Christ, who fulfills not only the book of Isaiah, but God's divine plan of salvation for us. Isaiah exclaims, "Behold!" And "behold" we must. It is as we behold these words effected through the Gospel that we discover not only the meaning of Lent, but the value of the Old Testament, for it prepares us for a confrontation with the love of God in the person of Christ.

I foretold it! I am Isaiah the Prophet, the son of Amoz. The Gospel exclaims it!

Christ was born of a woman while being the Son of God. He was born to suffer for man's sins upon the cross and born to triumph out of the grave. Listen to me!

(Bowing, hands outstretched) The Lord be with you.
(Congregation responds) And with thy spirit.
(Prayer)

Quotations used in this chapter: 2 Kings 19:32-35; Is. 7:13-14; 9:2-7; 53:2-12 NEB.
Other passages to consider for Scroll 1: Is. 52:7-10, 60:1-7; Scroll 2: Is. 42:1-9, 46:8-13, or 54:7-10.

BARTIMAEUS

Bartimaeus was blind, but sees clearly now and enjoys what he sees. His conversation is animated. He gestures excitedly, and speaks quickly but clearly about his encounter with the Lord. He is "sold" on the Savior and seeks to sell others.

His clothes should be bright, perhaps stripes. Sightless, dirt and color meant nothing, but now he is able to work, to be clean, and to enjoy lively hues.

A lectern in the center aisle at the foot of the chancel, draped in a bright fabric, should be his place of operation. He moves back and forth from the lectern freely. Bartimaeus is not stiff and formal, but relaxed and perfectly free. His joy is contagious.

Bartimaeus

Mark 10:46-52

(Enters, drinking in the vista in the darkened nave, straining to see!)

You'll forgive me if I stare from time to time. I can't help it, really. For long, lonesome, and dreary years I could not see the rounded, smiling faces of children, or look upon the wizened countenances of the elderly. For many a weary day I languished in the pitch of a bleak, personal night. I was blind, you see. *(Emphatically)* Blind! So grant me your pardon, if you catch me staring at your blinking eyelids or your curling lips! I'm fascinated yet by what I had missed all those years. The twinkle of youngsters' laughing eyes is still a sweet surprise to me. I marvel yet at the pliable expressions of people, who one moment frown, and the next beam with pride or happiness or cordiality. It's all so new to me, yet years of sight have gone their way too.

I am Bartimaeus. There is nothing particularly important about me, I suppose. I was blind, you see, like so many. I had no job, no property . . . nothing to call my own but the misery of my blindness and the bitterness of my loneliness. I begged for the spare coins of the rich to buy a loaf of bread to chew. I begged for discarded rags to keep me warm in the wintry chill. I begged for the scraps thrown from the tables of the well-to-do. I cried for the mercy of every passerby, but few spoke to me. Few gave me more than a penny. My only friends were the other blind ones I stumbled on along the highway that led from my town to Jerusalem.

Jericho had many beggars. There were whitened lepers, crippled people of every age, sick and deaf and blind. There were lunatics also, who raved and raged and ran rampant along the streets.

My ears became my eyes. I could see by sound where I was going or who was near. You learn to listen carefully to every rustle of the breeze. If you hear the swish of silk, it may mean a piece of silver in your cup. If you hear the leather slap of a guard's whip, or a soldier's uniform, it may mean a merciless beating is at hand. If you have no eyes with which to see, you must use your ears.

And so I did.

I had heard of a rabbi from Nazareth who worked wonders and preached a new and thrilling word of hope. They said He healed many a soul and had raised the dead. I heard whispered that His love knew no limits, that His eyes sought out the lonely, hurting, pathetic souls, and blessed them with His love. The name Jesus was common in our town, but the name of Jesus of Nazareth was an uncommon wonder in a city used to spectacular sights and famous names. After all, Joshua had made Jericho the prize of the Israelites centuries before, and other famed warriors and popular prophets had made it a way station as they ventured to Jerusalem.

So it was that Jesus was in town, the Nazarene, who some said was the Messiah. When you're a blind beggar, you leap at any straw of promise, and so my heart beat faster thinking this worker of miracles could say a few words of magic and transform my blindness into sight.

Whatever He was or could be, I chose to believe it . . . I placed Him above any bitterness I felt, any resentment I had. I put Him in the place of hope in my life. That's why I cried to Him when the street crowds began murmuring about His approaching party.

"Jesus," I shouted. (I cared not who heard me. I only hoped He would.) "Jesus, Son of David, have mercy on me!"

The indignant crowds told me to shut my mouth. Some taunted me with unkind words because I called Him "Son of David." Others, I guess, were embarrassed that a ragged beggar would sully the prestige of Jericho by yelling at so prominent a rabbi as Jesus. But I yelled all the louder, again and again, "O Son of David, have mercy on me!" I yelled with the voice that I had for the sight I had lost. I cried out with my whole being, for I was not to be cheated of this opportunity of meeting the One whose fame was so well known. I didn't know for sure who He was, but I had heard enough to believe Him to be the One sent from God. What powers He had . . . be they magic or something else . . . I could not know. I just knew He possessed what I had to have, and so I shouted until He heard me.

Jesus stopped. He said, "Tell him to come here." And so the people around me called me from my roadside perch. "You lucky fellow," some said. "Come on," they urged, "He's calling you!"

So overjoyed was I that I leaped from my spot and tore off my ragged cloak and went to Jesus as the people gently pushed, guiding me to the spot where He stood.

And then He asked me, "What do you want Me to do for you?" He asked the question no one had ever asked of me before; no one had cared enough before, no one had seen beyond my rags and beggarly attire to the deep need of my heart. I was physically blind, but so many had been socially blind to me. They hadn't even seen me, but Jesus had heard and had seen me both.

"O Teacher," I pleaded, "I want to see!" "I want to see!"

Swiftly, without further discourse, the Master said to me, "All right, it's done. Your faith has healed you." Instantly, like a cellar rat meeting the full force of a bright shaft of light, I was blinded with vision. I could see, and yet I couldn't. (Gesturing) I rubbed my eyes. What I had hoped would happen did, and I could scarcely believe it. For an instant I saw those around me . . . their amazed looks, their skeptical frowns, their curious glancing . . . but then my eyes met His and I knew what I had hoped and dared to believe was not miss-begotten. *(Joyously)* I saw Jesus and I followed Him down the road.

You see, Jesus was on His way to Jerusalem. The time had come. He knew what lay before Him . . . Gethsemane, Calvary, the sepulcher! He knew His Messianic role was coming to its fruition, but He stopped for one brief, hope-filled, wondrous moment to give sight to Blind Bartimaeus, the son of Timaeus. Nothing could stop Him from going to the cross for He knew what had to be done, yet His love was so complete and so marvelous that it made one last healing possible before He strode the last 15 miles to the city of His destiny.

I wonder how many of you suffer a blindness that you fail to realize. I wonder how many of you fail to cry to Jesus for healing of your sightless stumbling. Some of you are blind to the needs of the lonely. You don't care, but they do. Some of you are blind to the troubles of those who share with you the same street curb. When they gasp for help, crying blindly for Jesus, perhaps unknowingly, but nevertheless seeking Him, you drown out their plea with stifling words. "Now, now, don't cry. You're just upset!" In a way, some of you "shut up" the pleading voices of little children who want to know more but are thwarted because you fail to lead them to the Savior. Young men stretching out into manhood . . . young women reaching toward maturity . . . they sometimes are sacrificed by those who try to cover up their needs. There are more blind people in this world than those who cannot see.

If you are troubled, shout for Jesus to hear. Cry, as I did, "Jesus, Son of David, have mercy on me," and He will. Let no one keep you from making Him hear your inner need. Let no one prevent you from leaping to your feet, casting aside the rags of a past life to feel His healing power. Let no one deter you from following after Him down the road to Jerusalem, to Gethsemane, to Calvary, and to the emptied grave.

The love of Jesus is so great that it hears the cries of those who believe; and by His love at the pronouncement of His word, the miracle of healing instantly occurs. Faith in Christ will heal you too.

Most of you will forget what you've heard this night. You will think of me as some phenomenon of nature, rather than the blind man the Savior healed. You will try to explain away the miracle with some flashy logic to thus innoculate yourself from the faith that saves. But let me give you one last word: When you have lived in the squalor and filth of poverty; when you have led a visionless life in which you have not seen the flowering of the desert after the winter's abundant rains, or watched children frolic about the neighborhood, or perceived the splendor of brilliant colors . . . an azure sky, a snow white peak, a crimson rose, or a vermillion sunset . . . when you have been blinded to all of these miracles of God only to experience them in one instant at the Lord Christ's behest, you cannot dismiss Bartimaeus as some fraud of Scripture, some freak of nature. You see him fully to be what he is . . . a sightless man that Jesus loved and gave more than a vision of this world in which we live, but a man to whom He gave the vision of what it means to believe . . . perhaps blindly . . . yet knowingly.

(With excited joy) Look at me! I can see! I see Jesus as Lord and Savior. I see eternity with Him. What do you see? Or do you see at all?

Quotations: Mark 10:47-52 LB.

JOHN THE BAPTIST

John is no timid mouse. He asserts himself with fiery appeal. His seeming impudence is coarse, perhaps, but it matches his dress and his experience. He is no reed easily shaken by the wind, no man of "soft raiment," but a man of the desert, crudely dressed, but serious about his mission. He prepares the way.

John the Baptist's costume should match the description in St. Matthew 3:4 ff. Coarse burlap makes a fine tunic. Search around in secondhand clothing stores for something resembling "camel's hair," or a piece of fur-like cloth may be dyed to fit the bill. Look for remnants. A leather girdle and a crude staff and shoeless feet will complete the costume.

John needs no "setting." A lectern strategically placed at the front of the church in the center aisle will give him a place from which to operate.

When John enters, it should be from the rear of the darkened church, down the center aisle. Along the way John preaches to the congregation, "Turn from your sins . . . turn to God . . . etc." His voice is strong, stern, uncompromising. He is calling men to repentance and not to a tea party. Let the genuine John of Scripture be seen in your portrayal.

He exits as he came in, down the center aisle, preaching "Repent!" and "Believe!" as he walks aided by his staff. Both the opening and closing statements, which are from the Living New Testament, should be memorized.

John the Baptist

Luke 3:1-20

(*Sternly*) "Turn from your sins . . . turn to God . . . for the kingdom of heaven is coming soon."

"I hear a shout from the wilderness, 'Prepare a road for the Lord—straighten out the path where He will walk.'"

Repent! "Turn from your sins!"

(*Stopping in middle of church, John turns, points, accuses*) "You sons of snakes! Who said that you could escape the coming wrath of God?"

"Turn from your sins . . . turn to God . . . for the kingdom of heaven is coming soon."

"With water I baptize those who repent of their sins: but Someone else is coming, far greater than I am, so great that I am not worthy to carry His shoes! He shall baptize you with the Holy Spirit and with fire. He will separate the chaff from the grain, burning the chaff with never-ending fire, and storing away the grain."

"Turn from your sins . . . turn to God!" (*stern-eyed, pointing a finger*)

(*At the lectern, stern-eyed, pointing a finger*) How easy it is to see your need. Your eyes betray your docile exterior. They flash with the embarrassment and hurt of evil. How smugly you cloak your wrongdoing behind a quiet and dignified composure. But your eyes betray you. I see in your eyes the desire of something better than a life rotting from allegiance to the devil.

(Pleading) "Turn from your sins . . . turn to God!"

Escape to the desert . . . get away from the endless circle of confusion and heartache. Take time to think and study and pray. Converse with God! Meet His Son! Repent! When you return you will see how plain are the lines of sin upon the faces of others that you meet, but you will have erased yours by faith in the One who comes to save us.

(Contemplatively) There's something invigorating about a stay in the desert! With no one else but God to talk to, you get down to the bare essentials of life. I haven't wasted my life in this wilderness, eating whatever I could find . . . tasty wild honey straight from the hive; roasted grasshoppers minus their wings. I could have eaten more sumptuous fare in the houses of the rich, but I chose the simple foods of the desert to sustain life so that I could commune with God.

You can see that I am a man of simple tastes. Camel's hair keeps me warm in the night's chill. I need no luxuries. My mission is to preach the coming of salvation and not to lounge upon easy couches reveling in drunkenness.

I came to ready the world for my cousin, who is more than a blood relative to me, because He is my Lord and Savior. I was baptizing my followers in the river Jordan for cleansing from sin, when the Messiah came to me. The practice of my people is to baptize Gentiles, one of three requirements to become a convert to Judaism. The other two are circumcision and the offering of sacrifice. But I insist that so-called "clean" Jews as well as "unclean Gentiles" need the washing of repentance. And so I baptized them. But Jesus commissioned a baptism that was even more meaningful, a sacrament in which God enters into the life of the soul being baptized to forgive sins, to promise eternal life, to make a member within Christ's Church, and to make that person God's child.

This Jesus I have seen. He is the Messiah. He has come. He asked me to baptize Him. I protested. Why should I, a sinner, baptize Him who is without sin? "I am the one who needs to be baptized by You," I said.

But Jesus insisted. "Please do it," He said, "for I must do all that is right." So I baptized Him. And as we walked from the river, the heavens were opened to Jesus and the Spirit of God came down in the form of a dove. "And a voice from heaven said, 'This is My beloved Son, and I am wonderfully pleased with Him.'"

This is God's Son! Honor Him! Repent! "Turn from your sins . . . turn to God . . . for the kingdom of heaven is coming soon."

I am the son of a priest. Zechariah is my father; Elizabeth, Mary's cousin, is my mother. I could have been a priest also, but God called me to ready the highway of His Son, to work the hearts of men so that they would be receptive to the Messiah's message. The almighty God sent me preaching! Some say I rant and rave like a madman! Is there anything sane about evil? I am compelled to preach against it, to proclaim God's mercy and invite men to meet His Son.

I am older than the Lord Christ, yet He was before me. I was born before His birth in Bethlehem by six months, still He not only outranks me, but having come from God, He always was and still is. "I am not the Christ." I am not Elijah. "I am [but] a voice from the barren wilderness, shouting as Isaiah prophesied, 'Get ready for the coming of the Lord!'"

Some questioned my right to baptize. "I merely baptize with water," I said, "but right here in the crowd is Someone you have never met, who will soon begin His ministry among you, and I am not even fit to be His slave." That happened at Bethany, on the other side of the Jordan. It was the next day when Jesus was coming toward me that I told my followers, "Look! There is the Lamb of God who takes away the world's sin. He is the one I was talking about when I said, 'Soon a man far greater than I am is coming, who existed long before me!'"

I knew Jesus was the Messiah because "at the time God sent me to baptize He told me, 'When you see the Holy Spirit descending and resting upon someone — He is the one you are looking for. He is the one who baptizes with the Holy Spirit.' I saw it happen to this man, and I therefore . . . [testified] that He is the Son of God."

Repent! Repent!

Jesus is the Lamb of God. Andrew, my disciple, became His disciple. He brought his brother Peter to the Lord. Whom have you brought? What about your brother?

I am but a feeble voice crying to the world of men. Many have followed me . . . the sick and aged, the poverty classes, and the deeply troubled. They hear me, and follow . . . repentant, believing; but rich men turn deaf ears. They refuse to hear. I'm too rough, uncouth they say. I'm a radical, my message too extreme. My voice is drowned out by the rattle of their wealth, by their allegiance to things rather than to God. The Pharisees and Sadducees, educated, rich . . . religious men . . . they ignore me! But the message is universal. It's for you. Some of you will try to ignore me too, but my voice will haunt you, for I cry for repentance.

Give up your loyalty to evil. Follow Christ!

You hide your sins so cleverly beneath the facade of respectability. But God sees them. I see them too. They're written all over you. I see the eyes of cheats. I see the eyes of gossips. I see the eyes of those dominated by earthly passions. I see those who serve Satan rather than God . . . those who yield to temptation rather than faith . . . those who submit themselves to the forces of evil rather than the power of good. Repent! Turn to God . . . turn from your sins . . . the kingdom of heaven is coming soon. Let the Messiah . . . Jesus . . . take your sin, cleanse your hearts, and make you new.

The desert sun bakes you; Zechariah's son shakes you; God's Son saves you. The night wind whistles awesomely . . . its tune is sharp, penetrating . . . dissonant. *(Mocking the sound of the wind)* Repent, it cries . . . repent! Turn from your sin! Turn to God! Jesus brings melody to our lives, for He brings God's love. He takes our sin, and gives us love.

(Exits) The only way to get it, sinners, is to take it . . . by faith. Repent! Believe! "Repent, for the kingdom of heaven is upon you!" I am "a voice crying aloud in the wilderness, 'Prepare a way for the Lord; clear a straight path for Him.'" "Look! There is the Lamb of God who takes away the world's sin!"

Quotations: Matt. 3:2-17 LB; John 1:20-34 LB; Matt. 3:2-3 NEB.

MATTHEW

Matthew is dressed in the tradition of the day, a tunic and cloak, if desired, with sandals. The setting is more important than the costume. A high-leg desk (similar to the "guest book desk" or "usher's desk" found in many narthexes) is at an angle in the chancel. A high stool is behind it. A large earthenware jar, some scrolls and old account books may be at the foot of the desk to lend atmosphere of a tax office.

Two money bags, which can be made out of odds and ends of cloth, filled with money, are on the desk. Metal or plastic coins may be used, or gas station contest tokens, etc., may be used.

Matthew was a rough and tough businessman whose life and personality were sweetened by Christ and His Gospel. Once a crafty wheeler-dealer, he is now a pleasant person who can be thoroughly trusted.

Matthew

Matthew 9:9

(Standing at desk) It seems like a long time ago that I sat at this desk. Here I collected the custom tax from tradesmen who plowed their way along the overland route between Damascus to the northeast and the Mediterranean Sea to the west. It was a long time ago, and many things have happened since; yet had it not been for the fact that I sat at this desk I may have never known the joy I know today. I do a lot of reminiscing about that!

I'm a Jew and proud of it, but I worked for the Romans. My Jewish compatriots despised me for it, but I didn't care. I had it made. To be a tax collector was a disgusting thing to the devout. They hated the Roman conquerors with a passion, but they hated the Jews who served them even more. Roman law made it possible for us to exact whatever revenue we could get from the unsuspecting citizens, just as long as the Romans got their cut. The more the Jews vented their hatred of me, the higher the tax rose! My motto was "You'll pay for your contempt," and pay they did . . . dearly.

I had no fear. If they gave me trouble, we have a sizable Roman garrison in Capernaum to take care of their indignation and their protests. To pay a high tax was better, my Jewish clients reasoned, than to spend one night in a Roman jail.

Ah, Capernaum! What a delightful city. It has everything. We have the Sea of Galilee at our doorstep, and the rugged mountains around us. The Jordan flows into the sea but a short 2 miles away. We aren't far from Magdala or Bethsaida. However, Cana is a tiring 25 miles journey to the west, and Nazareth another 10 miles further to the south. But who needs to go there? In our town, we have manufacturing to attract the hardy workmen, and a wide array of shops in which villagers barter with the traders from Syria and Rome, Macedonia and Egypt.

Jesus came often to Capernaum. He would retreat to the hills outside of town when the bustle of city life drained His energies. The peaceful hills afforded Him quiet and inspiration. There He meditated, and in the hills He often preached. At other times the crowds would push Him into the sea as they crowded about Him to hear Him preach.

"No one can serve two masters; for either he will hate the one and love the other," Jesus said once, "or he will be devoted to the one and despise the other. You cannot serve God and mammon." I had heard Jesus say that on the Horns of Hattin, and I copied it in my book. It's true. You cannot serve the righteous God and a conniving devil simultaneously. Jesus showed me my purpose for being and gave to me insights into faith that I had never had before. He taught me the power of love, the wonder of forgiveness, and the sublime joy of letting Him carry the impossible burdens of sin and guilt I bore.

(Tossing money into aisle) I am one of His disciples. I don't suppose you knew that. To be sure, I didn't start out that way. I was one of the devil's own. I loved money and what it could buy. (Toying with coins) A tax collector may not have many *reputable* friends, but his wealth

attracts quite a crowd anyway. We weren't very religious. We would have been turned out of the synagog anyhow. We weren't welcome there. The religious ones lumped us together with harlots and lepers and other sinners. To them we were unclean, and maybe we were. I stole, just as the others did. The only difference between tax collectors and others, the decent citizens, is that we stole openly . . . their's was under the counter stuff.

While I served Rome, I led a merry life. We had a rich time . . . good food, good drink . . . women! I blush with shame to say it now. We led a merry life, but there was no joy. I had this gnawing ache within, this troublesome pain and cavernous emptiness. I put it down as loneliness and ordered more wine.

Jesus put His finger on my problem. I had seen Him several times and even went out to hear Him preach in the hills once or twice. At first it was only a lark. Everyone was talking about what He had to say. They told of miracles and a lot of other stuff that I found hard to swallow. I guess I thought He would entertain me on an otherwise dull day, but He got me to thinking. I knew what I thought was loneliness was something more. It was guilt.

Then I put up my defenses. I accused Him of being a religious fanatic, who wanted to turn the world upside down with His new ethics. He talked about love! Love! He said God loved us! What a laugh, I thought. If He loved me, why did I have this grubby job? Why did He let the sick die and the poor go hungry? Why did He let the Romans take over our country and deprive our freedom? Why did He let those hypocrites run the Temple? I was bitter. I didn't know what love was.

(Moving to congregation) I fought Him every inch

of the way, but there was something in His eyes, something in His voice, something within His very being that communicated to me the vast emptiness within, and the great filling power He had to give. He looked at me, and I knew how unbearable my loneliness, how shallow my life. I realized my sin.

And then one day He passed by my tax table. He looked at me and said, "Follow Me!" As if transfixed by the power of God that emanated from within His personality, I could not restrain myself. I got up and followed.

I didn't even balance my books that day. I followed, and I have no regret. Someone else took over my office, but more importantly, from that moment on Someone else took over my life.

(Returning to the desk) I had to celebrate. I asked my Lord to be the honored guest at a banquet, and He graciously accepted. I thought He might decline. After all, I was a tax collector . . . but He willingly came. Zealously, I invited all my friends. We had a houseful to meet Him. They all came. Curious, I suppose. I had hopes they too would follow Him. They were people like me . . . empty . . . He could fill them too.

For that banquet I had three things in mind. First I meant it to be a kind of celebration. I was so happy about having entered a whole new way of life. And secondly it was to be a kind of farewell, too, a formal announcement to my friends that I was no longer in business, certainly not in the mean and crooked business of sinking the talons of the Roman eagle into the tender flesh of my own countrymen. Most of all, though, it was a kind of desperate attempt to get the others to come along with me. Wistfully, and foolishly I suppose, I hoped that my former friends, meeting Jesus at the dinner table, sitting down with Him later for a long talk, might become His disciples too. Maybe, in those early days of my discipleship, I hoped to revolutionize the whole crooked tax collecting business overnight! Something I did accomplish, I know. They came, those friends of mine, utterly astonished at the step I had taken; they came ready to call me a complete fool. But they were eating my food and drinking my wine. They were polite enough, while partaking of my hospitality, not to laugh out loud or to scold me too severely. They left, I know, with a new respect for the Master. They left knowing that everything He told them was true. They left, and they didn't follow Him only because they were unwilling to pay the price.

I don't know if I was really willing to pay the price or not. It didn't seem to matter and still doesn't. I wouldn't allow myself to fall back into the old temptations, the old rutted pattern of life. I wanted what Jesus and He alone could offer me. Salvation!

(Pause while thinking) (Chuckle) I don't mean to laugh, but I would give anything to have a painting of the crowd of long-faced, righteously indignant souls who stood outside my home and looked aghast at the Rabbi from Nazareth coming into a tax collector's home. It's too bad they missed the point! That's what Jesus meant by love. *(Growing serious)* No one was beneath His loving them . . . no one, not even me. And certainly not you.

They had called me "Levi," which means "joined." I had been tied up with everything that was cruel and bad. I had been joined to cheating and extortion. When Jesus entered my life, I took a new name. I became Matthew. Matthew! It means "gift of the Lord," and that's what I had . . . the Lord gave me the gift of freedom. He saved me! What a gift to have . . . saved by the love of God!

I've said far too much about me. I reminisce too much these days. I'm concerned about you. How empty some of you look! You look worse than a tax collector's unfilled till. But I see a sparkle here and there. I see a glint of Christ in the eyes of a few that betrays the austere look they wear. How about you? Have you experienced the gift of the Lord in your life? He says "Follow me" to all of us. I'm not alone. He wants you to follow Him wherever you are—to be His disciple. Are you a salesman? He doesn't want you to leave your profession. He wants you to glorify Him through it. Are you a nurse or a teacher or parent or soldier? Let the gift of God's love for you make of your profession a temple in which God is worshiped and His love is shared with all that you meet.

(Holding up a money bag, jingling it) Are your fingers sticky like mine were? Do they cling to money that is another's? *(Take bag, empty it on desk)* Do you hide from God and pride yourself on your arrogance, your personality's power, your material prosperity? Are you content pushing others around, or to be pushed around? Are you happy . . . happy inside, in here? *(pointing to his heart)* "Happy are those who claim nothing," says our Lord, "for the whole earth will belong to them." Happy, too, are those whose business is not of the devil, but speaks the goodness of God, who throw out their idols and follow Jesus.

I penned a book a long time ago in which I sought to tell my Jewish friends what Jesus taught. Men have read it all over the face of the earth . . . not because I wrote it . . . but because they too have known emptiness as I did, and want to be filled.

I could tax the last penny out of the most arrogant businessman. Today I don't seek to tax him and close his account but instead to open his heart.

Believe me. I'm Matthew, a disciple, and what I have experienced is literally the Gospel truth! Amen.

Quotations: Matt. 6:24; 9:9 RSV; Luke 5:27 RSV; Matt. 5:5 Phillips.

CAIAPHAS

The costume of the high priest is not easily assembled, nor cheaply rented. It can cost a minimum of $35 to rent an authentic outfit . . . for one day! Therefore the best policy is to concentrate on the character and play down the costume.

If being authentic is your bag, numerous publications carry pictures of the high priest's vestments, which you can try to copy. Another way is simply to put Caiaphas in a tunic and robe, combining parts of other costumes already used so that it isn't altogether familiar. Sandals and a beard with the distinctive priestly headgear are helpful, but unnecessary.

A patio bench or a draped chair, not too fancy however, is all the equipment you need in addition to a lectern (small table with a binder to provide tilt for your manuscript will do).

The last portion of the portrayal is delivered standing, closer to the congregation. It can be memorized or another lectern of normal height provided.

Caiaphas is sure of himself, or appears to be, until near the end when he shows his own doubts. Don't fear being a little dramatic with any of the portrayals, but work to make them convincing. Caiaphas enters and exits from the chancel.

Caiaphas

Matthew 26:3-4

(Enter on last words of hymn, scolding) What's this thundering racket I hear in the palace? Can't a person rest without all this wailing and screaming?

Oh, now I know who you are. You're followers of that blasphemer Jesus. Well, you can just run along from here. I want nothing from you, and you will receive nothing from me. You cause nothing but trouble. Spouting your pious slogans and infecting the whole of Jerusalem with the vermin of your faith, you are nothing but agitators. A disease! That's what you Jesus-followers are . . . a disease!

(Hand to head) (Angrily) Oh my head! Now, see what you've done. You've given me a headache . . . a beastly, penetrating, throbbing headache. Let me sit down.

(Muttering, holding aching head) Life has been one murderous headache, one skull-splitting, mind-blistering headache. You would think a priest would be rid of such common maladies, but God does not relieve us. You would think that a high priest would not have to cope with such useless disorders! While the peasants run clear-headed and free, I suffer the pangs of a pulsating skull.

(Look up, accusingly) And you Jesus-followers are

largely to blame. It was enough to be high priest, to wear the breastplate of the tribes and the miter of the chief priest. To counsel the political leaders and keep peace with Rome, these were headaches also, but simple matters compared to the frustration that the so-called "King of the Jews" has given me.

Now mind you, it was expedient that one man should die for the people. You have to know something of psychology and mob hysteria in order to understand. With all the rumors abroad in Jerusalem, we could have had one hellish time here. A bloodthirsty revolt was afoot, but crucifixion put down any attempt at overthrowing Rome. Had a revolt been started by you *(sneering)* Jesus-lovers, the Roman army would have strengthened their own hand to end the revolt. They would have put to death those of us who have slaved to keep an amiable peace. I told the other priests and the Pharisees, "Let this one man die for the people—why should the whole nation perish?"

You clever schismatics! You thought of my words as a prophecy! You considered it *(mockingly)* "a prediction that Jesus' death would not be for Israel only, but for all the children of God scattered around the world." Idiots! Stupid men! Morons! We outwitted you, you fools!

(Proudly) We plotted His death, and it wasn't difficult!

For every leader has his foes right within his circle of friends. All we had to do was locate the weakest link in Jesus' "council of the twelve," and the deed was as good as done. Haven't you found that to be true? There is always a Judas available in every administration who is ready to sell his hero for a bag of gold, a few pieces of silver, or a place of prestige in another regime. We found our man. It was not hard.

You pious fools! You say that a high priest should not stoop to such a crime, but let me tell you that I am God's emmissary here, and thus I know what it is He wants of me.

It is not a crime to rid society of its infections, now it is? Jesus was an infection. He was poisoning the minds of people. They even said He raised a man from the dead . . . Lazarus of Bethany, I believe it was. Well, now we can't have distortions like that paralyzing the minds of the people, now can we? Thus I served the people well pushing Jesus toward the cross.

(With exasperation) Why the numbers in the Nazarene's sect continue to multiply is beyond me. You don't rub out disease so easily, I guess, but if I had my way, there would be a little more blood-letting and we'd have done with this religious cancer. Why the sales in the Temple stalls have fallen off sharply! Some of the merchants and the money changers not only lost a good share of their inventory when that Man Jesus took a whip to them the day after His supposed "triumphal" entry into Jerusalem, but their business has dropped to just a dribble of what it was. The Jesus-lovers say they don't have to make sacrifices in the Temple any longer. They say He is the "Lamb of God" who atoned for the sins of men on the cross.

I'll show you who is the "Lamb of God!" *(Threatening)* If you people don't get back to your religious duty and follow the Law I'll impose serious sanctions upon you. How do you like that? Yes, yes, I think that might be a good idea. Economic sanctions, religious sanctions, civil sanctions . . . yes, I'm sure you'll change your tune then.

Oh, my head!

Jesus was bad enough! But who do these men, Peter and John, think they are? They continue to disturb the people, I'm told. We'll deal harshly with them as well. They claim Jesus to be the Messiah! They blaspheme also.

(Listening) What's that? What do you say? The grave? What grave? Oh, His grave? No, no, it wasn't empty. Don't believe those rumors. They're false, false, I tell you.

(Stammering) The—er—a—er—guards said friends of Jesus came and stole His body. Yes, the tomb was sealed. But they stole His body, I tell you! He's not the Messiah! He can't be. After all, the Messiah would not be a carpenter's son. He wouldn't be dressed in peasant clothes. He would be regal in splendor. He would ride victorious over the heathen Romans. This Jesus can't be . . . He isn't . . . the Messiah! The empty grave is all a hoax!

Now you must go. My head aches and I must rest. Be off with you before I call the guards.

(Rising, moving toward the congregation he speaks to himself, quietly)

What if I took my position too seriously? What if this Jesus is God's Son as He says? What if the people find out that we bribed the guards to say His body was stolen while they were asleep? What if they discover that the guards even fainted at the presence of a so-called angel at the grave? What if they discover that I'm but an empty shell, a frightened, uncertain, embittered, disturbed old man?

(Desperately) Jesus, what have I to do with you?

It isn't my fault that He had to die! It had to be. Didn't the other priests agree with me and issue the verdict of death? What a headache He has been to me, and what a headache I have been to those who would believe.

(With artificial pride) I am Caiaphas Joseph, high priest of the Jews. My word is God's! *(To himself)* Why is it I feel that maybe His Word should be mine?

Oh, my aching head!
(Exit)

Quotations: Matt. 27:11, 37 RSV; John 11:50, 52 LB; John 1:29 RSV.

PAUL

Paul is a very real person. His piety seems natural and unaffected. No soap opera character, Paul prays and witnesses freely with dramatics, but concern is evident. He speaks freely with God not because of any supposed intimacy, but out of a very real, long-standing relationship.

A simple tunic with a bright sash and sandals is Paul's costume. He is chained, however, both hands and feet. You can buy chain by the yard in most hardware stores at a reasonable price. Fix the loops for hands and feet so that they may be slipped on easily, but will not slip off during the portrayal.

For the setting use a picnic table bench covered with a white cloth on which the manuscript is placed. Set the bench at an angle in the chancel so that as Paul enters and nears the bench he may appear to have been pushed, and stumbles toward the bench where he remains in a kneeling posture.

In the nave by the front row, and behind a pew screen, arrange a lectern. You may place manuscript there to refer to as Paul talks to Demetrius.

The prayer at the end is to be a free prayer, if possible, in which Paul remembers those struggling in prisons of stone and doubt and asks that they may be opened to the Gospel.

You may want to have a water jug by the bench to add to the atmosphere.

Paul

Acts 9:1-25

(Enters from front, stumbles, kneels in prayer by a bench)
Here I am, Lord, jailed again like a common thief.

And what have I stolen? You know, Lord. I have stolen souls from the clutches of the devil. I have ransacked his following and come off with quite a number of jewels this time. You will make of them, these uncut yet willing stones, sparkling gems for the King's crown. Their brightness will attract even more eyes to the cross of Christ, for these souls are willing to serve You no matter the cost, Lord.

Jailed again! What number is it this time? I've lost count. Between imprisonments and beatings, you have led me on a merry adventure through one danger after another. But you have always led me. I have been beaten by the Jews five times the forty-lashes-less-one. And then, as if for a change of pace, I have been beaten three times with rods. What will it be this time? No matter. You strengthen me, Lord. You give me courage. You inspire determination, persistence, faith. Thanks for leading me, Lord, to the place where I am and the job that needs doing.

Three times I have been shipwrecked, and once I was adrift at sea a day and a night. In fording flooded rivers and plagued by robbers, I have criss-crossed this world rescued by you so often I cannot begin to number the times. Hunger and thirst, toil and hardship, cold and exposure, all these have I known. Lord, I boast not of the difficulties, but the victories. For every calamity, there has been a triumph. For every burden, there has been uncovered another jewel for the Kingdom. There's Timothy and Silas and Mark ministering . . . what gems they are! *(Pause)*

How long has it been since you changed my direction? The years have taken their toll, but I feel as invigorated now as I did that day you knocked me to the ground by your radiant holiness by that flash of light, that holy vision! There was I, on my way to Damascus to teach the Christians a lesson. I had the necessary credentials to take any Jesus-believer bound hand and foot to Jerusalem to be dealt with by higher authority. How I loathed the Christians and their faith then . . . until you changed my mind. In the 3 days' blindness I experienced by the brightness of your appearing on the Damascus Road, I discovered how blind I had been.

I had been blind to Your love, O God; blind to Your mercy; blind to Gospel and the sacrifice of Christ. You know how to open the eyes of the blind, don't you Lord? You did it to me, and through me to a whole host of followers.

I'll not forget the Damascus Road. You called me; out of the heavens You called me. "Saul, Saul, why do you persecute me?" you asked.

"Who are you, Lord?" I responded with quavering voice.

"I am Jesus, whom you are persecuting; but rise and enter the city and you will be told what you need to do."

I did as you said, and discovered that my life had changed. Despite the fact I have a university education (trained at Tarsus) and sat at Gamaliel's feet, I had never been able to open my mouth to tell others about truth, about the Grace of God, until you opened my eyes to it. I proclaimed Jesus joyously then as now! "He is the Son of God," I told everyone. I hoped they wouldn't be as blind as I had been. You gave me strength to make the Gospel known. I went to my Jewish friends, but they turned from me. They couldn't believe what had happened to me. Some even plotted to kill me, but You saw me safely over the city wall in a basket. I escaped their murderous plot. Even Christ's disciples feared me when I got to Jerusalem. They thought it was a trick. The Hellenists wanted to argue and the Jews were angry. Still, Lord, you made my voice strong enough to reach into many souls. The Holy Spirit multiplied our efforts and before long our small throng became a mighty gathering.

And here I am, Lord, in jail again. *(Humorously)* I must plot my course more carefully! No telling how long I might be confined here. I've places to go and people to see. I've got a Gospel to proclaim, Lord, so show me what you want me to do here first before I shove on from here to another port . . . and another jail. *(Rising, he sits on the bench.)*

I noticed that young officer when they brought me in. Is he the one to whom you want me to reveal the Good News? How about that slave who scrubs the corridors? Is he one of those I'm to lead into the Way? Those fear-filled souls in the cell next to mine . . . they seem so frightened, so upset. Can they be the jewels in the rough you want mined in this cave? I have a feeling, my Jesus, that you're not sending me to one or the other, but to them all. Give me the words to utter and they shall be spoken.

My eyes grow dim. It's hard for me to read or write as

I used to, Lord. Every time I ask you about my malady, this "thorn in the flesh," you remind me of a truth I all too quickly forget. "My grace is sufficent for you, for my power is made perfect in weakness," You tell me. It's true, Lord, it's true. *(Kneeling again)*

Yet, write I must. Even Christians quarrel, I must settle their theological squabbles, so that they can get on with Kingdom business. They bicker over foolish things. They stalk out if things don't go their way. Give me patience and vision to see their need and fulfill it. I worry over the Christians in Corinth, that labyrinth of moral decay. What of young Timothy? How goes it with him, Lord? And, Lord, did Philemon receive Onesimus as his brother? He's his slave, yet, but he's more than that. In Christ, the two are brothers and should make serving you foremost. I pray that Philemon forgives his runaway, for he ran not so much to get away from Philemon as to serve Christ. He can do it within that household, and they together can glorify Your name.

You care, Lord, for the whole church. The Holy Spirit has called together souls in Derbe and Lystra, in Troas and Ephesus, Berea, and even sophisticated Athens. I know they praise you in Jerusalem, in Tyre and Sidon, and as far as Rome. *(Excitedly)* There's Spain, Lord, let me go to Spain and Carthage and Cyrene. Is it a wanderlust, I have, Lord, or is it your call I keep hearing. You called me from Asia Minor to Macedonia. You have called me every place I've been, and I've followed. Where do I go from here, Lord? Where? *(Long pause)*

I must not dream of other worlds to conquer. I have been given a world right here that needs hearing of your resurrection, Lord. "I am not ashamed of the Gospel; it is the power of God for salvation to every one who has faith, to the Jew first and also to the Greek." Bars and stone walls cannot keep conviction in prison; they cannot trap the Gospel, or keep love a captive. I have work to do, Lord—souls in need of saving! *(Rising)*

(Calling) Say, Jailer! I must tell you of my Lord Christ and His goodness! *(Pause)* Oh, perhaps another time then. You must hear, however. You must hear it!

(To another unseen person) The Lord be with you, friend!

I'm Paul, A Roman citizen by birth, a Christian by faith. I see you keep the cells clean. They call you Demetrius, do they? Then tell me, Demetrius, what grieves you? I can free you from your heartache; you know that, don't you. I can free you from grief and sorrow, from the overpowering control of Satan and his temptations. For in the words I can offer you, God will snip the chains of your soul from bondage to sin.

Freedom is where you are, Demetrius. You're free now! Because you are a slave, does not mean man can enslave your soul or imprison your mind. Let me tell you how Jesus Christ released my soul from the shackles of sin and hate. Let me tell you how God Himself filled my heart, aching with vengeance, to spilling over with love. *(With assuring conviction)* Demetrius, Demetrius. They have only my body, but my mind is free, my heart is at liberty, my soul is captive to no man. God sent His Son into the world that men like us might know what it's like to be free. He sent His Son to pay for our release, and pay He did. Not as they do at the marketplace, when a slaver sets up shop to dispose of his captives. This Jesus pays for sin another way. He was born of a virgin and lived as we do, but our Lord is God's Son, man's Redeemer. He atoned for our sins upon a wooden cross. It was a horrible death He died! On the third day He arose triumphant. The grave was empty; He was alive again. Many saw Him and many believed. They knew the Messiah, long promised to the Jewish nation, had come . . . He came not to save Jews only, but all men who by faith accept Him as their King. He came to save you, Demetrius.

He appeared to me in a vision on a highway one day when I was on my way to destroy the Christian church at Damascus. *(With joy)* That was a day, Demetrius. That was a day! Let Him into your heart—let Him in. He loves you and wants to transform your bitterness into beauty. He wants to free us all from sins, enslavement—who is not indignant over man's inhumanity, his materialism, and exploitation of the poor.

I hear the guard calling you, my son. Go for now, but we will speak of this again. First, let us bow our hearts in prayer and thank God that we have one another, for He has given you to me to encourage my spirit, and I have been given to you to save your soul by the Gospel of Christ.

(Free prayer for those struggling in prisons of stone and doubt)

Quotations: Acts 9:4-6, 20 RSV; 2 Cor. 12:7, 9 RSV; Rom. 1:16 RSV.

JUDAS

Judas is a man of changing moods. He switches from boastfulness to pathetic remorse. He is quick to accuse, but also swift to forewarn. Judas is a man frustrated by impatience and a goal that was less than what Jesus sought.

A simple black cassock, colorful sash, and a beard penciled on with an eyebrow pencil will add to the characterization. He needs a heavy rope noose and a stand for his speech, unless it is memorized. Drape a dark fabric about the lectern or stand to add to the dramatic effect of the monolog setting.

Judas should not be glued to the stand, but know his speech well enough that he may move freely at times. Don't be hesitant about getting into character. Play him as one who has returned for this very special visit with a Christian congregation, who is personally sensitive to the situation of the place he visits. This characterization will be most meaningful just before or during Holy Week.

The entrance may be from the chancel side. Walk firmly yet heavily toward the lectern. Pause to look at your audience as if weighing their similarity to the character you play. Then proceed with haughty spirit. As you leave the chancel, exit down the center aisle muttering quietly to yourself, "You must be different than I was." Repeat it until exiting to the narthex.

Judas

John 13:21-30

(With haughty spirit) You wouldn't expect people to turn out to see a traitor, would you: But they do! You came to see me, the most infamous betrayer of them all. Judas of Kerioth, son of Simon, a Judean and a disciple of Jesus!

People spit on my name! They have made an oath of it! They insult each other with it, and make me an example to be scorned, a subject to be condemned. I am loathed by many by their words, but praised by their deeds! You have given me a color to symbolize my betrayal. You have called me yellow, the color of dung.

And if you treat me so, why is it so many people show up when I'm around? Is it because they are not so different from me? *(Smiling deceitfully)* We are so much alike, you and I. No wonder you come in such large numbers to meet Judas!

I won't deny I betrayed Jesus. Betray Him I did. Can you deny that you have betrayed Him? As long as mankind hates, you betray the One who loves. As long as you deceive each other and cheat one another . . . as long as you maim and murder . . . you betray Him. As long as you make money your chief object of affection, and social position your main goal in life you are like me. Together we betray the One they call the Christ. We're not so different, are we? I am called "the betrayer," but I'm among friends, am I not? You have betrayed Him too! Yet Jesus chose me to be one of the Twelve. Not even Jesus wins them all! But He knew my destiny, before I was aware of it. "Did I not choose you, the Twelve," He said, "and one of you is a devil?" He knew. I could not fool Him. Nor can you. He knows how much like me you really are.

I am known for what I am, but you are clever to hide your inner feelings from public light. You're all like me. Don't deny it! I alone stand out as chief betrayer, however, for I forgot what the Lord Christ taught. I should have known that even one such as I could be forgiven. I was possessed by a Satanic force more evil than I can say. It blinded me from so much, but you have the chance to see. Yes, we're not so different. We all have betrayed Him, yet you have a chance to meet Love's power and know the cleansing might of forgiveness. Or have you too missed that truth?

(Boastfully) I am Judas, the only disciple to hold an office among the Twelve. I collected the receipts, banked them in my purse, and disbursed the sum for daily bread. The others were too busy with their ministering to people's spiritual needs to care for our own physical essentials. After all, we had to eat too! I kept it all in order. I have a mind for figures. I'm not one to pass a bargain by either. I like the ring of silver in my purse. Those Galileans could not match my ability to keep the books in balance. Were it not for me, they would have met financial chaos long before.

But you, too, have a penchant for figures. *(Accusingly)* I see I'm not alone in holding a tight grasp upon the purse. Why, even I gave more to the Lord's work in my few years with Him than many of you have given in a lifetime. I clutched those 30 pieces of silver as if it was a fortune meant for me, repayment for all I'd given. The stain of guilt that blood money showed burned within my hands. You clutch your wealth with far less guilt . . . and you have far greater resources than I did, and you do it with more than Judas-like allegiance to it. I'm proud of you . . . how tightly you keep your purse strings tied. You call it thriftiness, but I say it's greed . . . GREED! You're greedy like the one you hate, who stands before you.

Do you remember when Jesus visited the home of Simon the Leper at Bethany? Mary, Martha, and Lazarus' sister anointed Jesus' head and feet in an extravagant manner with expensive ointment from an alabaster jar. I protested the waste. It might have been sold for a large sum . . . and we could have used it. It could be given to the poor, I said. But Jesus saw my shallow argument and said she had done a beautiful thing. "You always have the poor with you," He said, "but you will not always have Me!"

You are like me, aren't you? I can see we think alike. You think it was a waste too! I can see I'm among friends. To throw money away on the body of Christ . . . what you Christians call the church . . . is a waste, isn't it? It's like Mary did. Jesus liked it, but I say it's a waste. Your giving, most of you, shows you think just like I do. Why give to missions? Why not help yourself, instead? Why befriend the poor or minister to the sick? Why build Sunday schools and churches or colleges or seminaries? It's a waste! Keep your money to yourself. I bear the name of contempt . . . Judas . . . yet you bear your name with respect, when we think so much alike. Ironic, isn't it?

Frankly, I was disappointed with Jesus. Oh, He was nice enough, but He lacked my militancy. Our country needed a rebel to break Rome's stranglehold. Jesus could have been the one. He was nice enough, yes, personable! I liked Him . . . despite everything, I like Him. He had a magnetic personality, but . . . well, you know . . . He was too slow-going for my taste. He wanted to preach all the time. Now don't get me wrong, I enjoy a good sermon once in a while. But what I wanted was action. He had such tremendous powers to heal people and even to control nature by His word; He could have led us out of bondage. I could have used His power. He could have become king and led the people against the Roman scourge, but no! He told Pilate, "My kingdom is not of this world!" He had some fantasy about a world after this one, a life beyond the grave!

The tragedy of my life is that I found out too late that it was not a fantasy. It was truth!

He knew what I would do. Even when we celebrated the Passover in that rented upper hall, He knew. I could see it in His eyes. And then He said, "One of you will betray Me!" I was nervous. I didn't want to give myself away, but the disciples persisted in asking Him who it might be. He said, "It is he to whom I shall give this morsel when I have dipped it!" And then He gave it to me!

Those stupid disciples! They didn't catch on. They thought, because I carried the money, that Jesus had told me to buy something for the feast, or to give something to the poor! Me? Give to the poor? Ha! But then I left.

I am Judas, and like my namesake, Judas Maccabees, who struck the first blow for religious freedom against Antiochus Epiphanes of Syria, the Seleucid king who controlled Palestine 200 years before me. I was out to overthrow my enemy Rome. I thought Jesus would be the leader. *(Defensively)* I offered to betray Him simply to make Him stand up and fight. I thought that would motivate Him. He seemed so slow in accepting the mantal I was sure to be His. He was missing all the opportunities. I thought I could motivate Him, but I learned instead that the devil had motivated me so that for thirty lousy pieces of silver—$20, no more—I handed Him over to those who would kill Him. I had hopes of playing both ends against the middle to gain the victory I craved. *(With remorse)* I had been used. Like a wrench in the hands of Satan I tightened the bolt upon the chains of slavery . . . spiritual as well as political. I was used!

(Boastfully) I could have handled the king's treasury, had my plan worked. I could have been in charge of national revenue and kept the books for a million people. *(Returning to remorse)* Instead, I expended my hope to become bankrupt of faith. I betrayed my Master for a wretched handful of silver. I gave Him a kiss and entrusted Him into the hands of murder.

And then in a flash *(snapping finger)* I saw all that I had done was as if I had been put in a trance. It made no sense. I had betrayed not only a friend but my country and my God as well. I repented of it, and brought back the money to the chief priests and elders. I told them, "I have sinned in betraying innocent blood."

They treated me with contempt. "What is that to us? See to it yourself!" *(Handle noose)* I threw down the filthy lucre and it clanked murderously upon the Temple floor. With it they bought the potter's field to bury strangers in, as the prophet Jeremiah had foretold. And I was first to be buried there . . . the victim of the noose. I despaired beyond consolation. I could see nothing but the utter shame of my crime and the condemnation of history. I should have sought the Lord. Peter did, and was forgiven. I could have been forgiven too, for God's heart is filled with love. But I could not even do that.

(Sorrow, then recover)

(With false pride) I am Judas Iscariot. There may be the hiss of the snake in my name, and the strong odor of the devil in my sin, but we're *so* much alike, you and I. So much alike! You scoff at me and scorn my evil, but what have you done to nullify your betrayal of the One who came to love? You are no less evil.

You people today are no different than the ambitious people of my day. You exploit the innocent. You become impatient with God and play your foolish little games of spiritual "hide-and-seek" or "I'm mad at God!" You hate the poor . . . as I did . . . who were a constant drain on our meager resources. "Why don't they help themselves?" you whine. I said the same thing. You match my hate for the Romans with your bigotry toward the minorities. You scratch after money with the same eagerness that I had in going after the 30 pieces of silver. You are eager for personal power. I, too, dreamed of becoming important in an earthly kingdom of Jesus. We're so much alike, but your end must not be like mine.

Satan may have my soul, but there's no need for him to have your's too. You have something . . . Someone to live for. *(Convincingly)* Jesus can effectively do to you what I wouldn't let Him do for me. He can transform your hardened heart. He can redirect your energies from the idols of wealth and power to the cause of sacrifice and service. He can change the world through you, if you'll let Him. As long as you are on your side of death, you have a chance. Christ has done all that needs doing. He smote the devil a decisive blow through His death and resurrection. You must do what I didn't do. You must believe Him.

It could have happened through me . . . a changed world! I repented of my shame, but not my sin. *(Picking up noose again)* I died in a noose of my own making, a suicide. How sad that such a man as I . . . one that could have been great in the Kingdom of God . . . should become so base in the history of the world! You are different. You must be different. You have opportunity to live in the grace of God.

You came to see a traitor, and a traitor I am. But if I could relive the past, I would quarrel with the devil and honor the Lord. Alas, history has been written. I cannot change the truth. I am pathetic, yes, but not to be pitied. I had my chance. Don't follow me! I fear for you, for we are so much alike. Don't betray the Master, for He is a king all right . . . the King of all that really matters. He's your Savior . . . the Savior of all who believe in Him. Would that I could still ask Him to be mine!

I am Judas.
I betrayed Jesus for 30 pieces of silver.
I betrayed Him with a kiss.
I see that I'm among friends.
You betray Him too!
    Is it for silver?
    You betray Him with a kiss?
You must be different than I was.

Quotations: John 6:70 RSV; Matt. 26:11 RSV; John 18:36 KJV; Matt. 26:21 RSV; John 13:26 RSV; Matt. 27:4 RSV.

PILATE

Pilate's costume may be made out of an old surplice or cotta. Simply stitch the sleeves, if they are pointed or rounded, inside the upper part of the sleeve. Wear a narrow cord or leather thong. A simple red cape that Pilate may flourish over an arm as he enters and exits may be attached to the shoulders with pins. A ring or two, a heavy chain and medallion about the neck (cheap costume jewelry to be found in nearly every home), and sandals will round out the costume. Study pictures of Pilate or other Romans of his time and fashion a simple costume that will add to the authenticity of the portrayal.

The setting is to be simple also. Set an occasional chair or even one of the throne-like clergy seats found in many chancels in the center front of the church. Spotlight it, if possible. Drape a bright fabric over the "throne" to add to the drama of the setting. Fashion a lectern that may be used while seated. Short table with a loose-leaf binder on top, draped with a piece of fabric, sheet, bedspread, or drape will also lend a bit of interest to the setting as well as utility. White notes will not show up as readily on white sheets, so that may be helpful in keeping the audience from awareness of reliance on notes.

Pilate still thinks of himself as an imperial governor. Occasional cracks in this exterior deception reveal his own weaknesses. Pilate may enter from the chancel side with military stride, quick and heavy-footed. He stands in the lower chancel, surveys the scene, making his opening speeches, and then retreats to the "throne." As the occasion demands, Pilate may lean forward, pointing his ring-cluttered finger for emphasis. He is a man very much aware he is the center of things . . . or was! Like the has-been movie star, Pilate cannot stop playing the role.

Pilate

John 18:29 ff.

(With an imperious attitude) So you want to visit with Pilate, do you?

There should be the sound of trumpets, the roll of the drum to announce my entrance. You should do what is fitting for a governor. Have you no understanding of diplomatic protocol?

Well, I see that you have a throne set for me. You have some considerations for my rank, at least. *(Straining to see)* And what is that beyond? An altar?

(Recalling) Oh, yes, this is what you Christians call Lent. I recall now. I recall the first Lent, the Thursday Jesus was betrayed, you call it Maundy Thursday. Had it not been for the events of that night and the day that followed, I would probably have been in Caesar's favor. Instead, one weak decision after the other dogged me into oblivion. Me! Pontius Pilate, once governor of Judea!

And what is that altar for? *(With curiosity)* Is it true what I have heard rumored about you Christians that you cannibalize little children? You call it a love feast, don't you, and eat flesh and drink blood? Is that true! I can't believe civilized people, even Jews, would do such a disgusting thing.

My wife Claudia Procula, had forewarned me about Jesus. She had a dream, you see. I remember her words to me, "Have nothing to do with that righteous man, for I have suffered much over Him today in a dream." And she had, but what could I do? I was the governor, and I had to listen to the petty disputes that arose among the Jews. I should have listened to her, for I have suffered greatly also because of that One's death.

Ordinarily I lived at Caesarea, where the balmy sea breezes kept us cool and comfortable from Palestinian heat. When the Jews celebrated their festivals, I moved to Jerusalem for there were bound to be riots and demonstrations there, and all manner of havoc. That's why I was in Jerusalem that particular week . . . it was Passover, a high celebration. That's why the chief priests and the elders of the people bound Jesus and brought Him to me.

I questioned Him. I gave Him His chance to speak. They accused Him of stirring up trouble from Galilee to Judea, but I could recall no trouble that He had caused, save maybe that little episode in the Temple a few days before. He drove those money-loving leeches out of the Temple! What a spectacle that must have been. I questioned Jesus, but He was not the most cooperative prisoner. He was tight-lipped. When the chief priests and the elders leveled their charges at Him, He refused to answer . . . not one word to a single accusation. He did admit to being some sort of king when I asked Him. "Are you the King of the Jews?" I inquired. "You have said so," was His reply. I offered this "King of the Jews" to the people but they didn't want Him.

I must admit that I wondered about Him. He was a strange man not to even defend Himself. He didn't have the criminal attitudes. He wasn't haughty or arrogant. He was a gentleman, yet He wouldn't open up to defend Himself.

(Defensively) What could I do? I sent Him to the Idumean, to Herod Antipas, the puppet ruler of Northern Palestine. After all, Jesus was a Galilean and belonged to Herod's jurisdiction, not mine. Why shouldn't he handle such a sticky issue? King Herod was in town for the Passover ritual. He was glad that I made the gesture, since we had been at odds with one another. When he returned Jesus to me, we became fast friends. *(Proudly)* You see what a little diplomacy can do? We found favor with one another . . . and in politics favor is an important find. Jesus was returned to me wrapped in a purple cloak with a crown of thorns on His head! That's Galilean justice for a Galilean King!

I thought by scourging Him that the Jews would be pacified, but they were not. They wanted me to release a criminal in place of Jesus. That, too, was one of those peculiar customs that the Jews claimed of Rome. A prisoner was to be released at Passover time. I offered to release Jesus, this self-styled but guiltless king. He was responsible for no crime, but they were intent on His murder. The chief priests were envious of Him, and His popularity I suppose. The crowd wanted Barabbas instead. He was a dangerous insurrectionist, a murderer!

What could I do? My hands were tied, and rather than have them sullied by that bloodthirsty mob's quest for a lamb to slay, I washed my hands of the matter. Why not? That cleansed me of any wrongdoing, and the crowd accepted the responsibility. You might term it "legalized murder," but it was the diplomatic thing to do. It prevented a disastrous riot. It may have even saved some lives. It was surely the expedient thing to do.

This audience recalls for me the beginning of the end when I judged Him! Not only the end for Jesus but for me as well.

It's strange to me that such a man as He should still be celebrated among people today. He was a simple man. He was not boastful. I would say He seemed kindly, thoughtful. He wouldn't have made much of a king. He was surely different from Herod Antipas, and far different from Caesar. Why the Jews feared Him I'm sure I'll never know. Fear Him, they did, however. And so He was crucified.

(*Pensively*) I wonder about Claudia's dream. Perhaps I should have stood my ground and offered Him the protection of my office. I wonder what He meant when He said, "You would have no power over me unless it had been given you from above; therefore he who delivered Me to you has the greater sin." He seemed to judge me, rather than I judging Him. Judas may have the greater sin, yet His inference and the stinging hint is that I too am guilty of His death. But what could I do? I did what seemed diplomatic . . . what appeared to be expedient. (*Pause*) What could I do?

(*Disturbed anew by the frailty of his plea*) I must declare this audience at an end! I thought I had buried the past, but you cannot hide the pains of wrongdoing.

Oh yes, before I go, you might be interested in knowing that something did happen that was indeed strange. After Jesus died on the cross and was buried, (*matter-of-fact manner*) the following Sunday morning His tomb was found to be empty. My guards reported the whole incredulous event to me. They had been set to watch over the tomb, which I ordered sealed in order that His body could not be stolen. There were other reports that many saw Him after that alive. Impossible dreams!

(Pensively again) But I have seen Him too! Not like the rest, mind you. I have seen Him in my dreams night after night. His innocent eyes haunt me. Claudia's dream has become mine. Like hers it troubles me greatly.

If there is anything I have to say to end the matter, it is this: Listen to your conscience, and even if there is a more expedient way to handle difficulty, resolve it with justice. Don't give in to cowardice. "Cowards die many deaths, the valiant die but once," they say.

What could I do? I did the best I knew how. It was the diplomatic, the expedient thing!

(Pause) The next time I come I shall expect a fanfare and the roll of the drum. Protocol is important. Kindly remember my rank! After all, I *was* governor of Judea.

(Exit)

Quotations: Matt. 27:19 RSV; John 18:33 RSV; Matt. 27:11 RSV; John 19:11 RSV.

CLEOPAS

The New English Bible provides the text used in this portrayal, the appointed text for Easter Vespers. This characterization may take place in the pulpit. If the pastor portrays Cleopas, he may take a length of cloth and drape it about himself, similar to outercloaks depicted in many Biblical works of art. There is no need for him to remove his vestments, and no need for him to use any drapery either unless he so chooses.

Cleopas' message fits a family service, a Sunday school Easter opening, or even a traditional service. The one portraying Cleopas should do his best to remember he is Cleopas for those few moments, and not the local pastor or councilman. Cleopas is humble—a nobody who becomes a somebody through Jesus. He must commute this exciting discovery by his own enthusiasm for Christ in an exceedingly convincing way for the portrayal to have the impact it can have.

There is no need for a "setting" since the pulpit is the place where Cleopas makes his witness to the congregation.

Cleopas

Luke 24:13-35

I am Cleopas, a disciple of Jesus.

I am not well known. You doubtlessly know the names of Peter and John, Matthew and Andrew, but my name is obscure. I'm a nobody. I was not one of the Twelve, but instead served the Lord whenever I could. My trade kept me busy, yet the words the Master spoke intrigued me. As often as He came to my village, I was there to hear Him. He had a wondrous way of telling us profound truths.

But I must continue my story. It's proper that I should be your guest on this festival, for it commemorates the event that made it possible for all nobodies to be somebody. I would still be unknown had it not been for that Resurrection victory of Christ.

My companion and I had been in Jerusalem for the Passover feast, but the days had been filled with sadness rather than gladness. The crowds that received Jesus like a king on Sunday shouting "hosannas" of praise, thrusting cloaks and palms in His path, were quick to seek His crucifixion. He had done no wrong, but they charged Him with all sorts of false accusations. It was a plot of the high priest Caiaphas and his stubbornly arrogant father-in-law Annas to kill Jesus. So great had Jesus' following become, they feared for their jobs. The Roman governor was not much better. He was indifferent to Jesus and His innocence. He let them murder Him, although he knew the Lord was innocent.

At any rate, Jesus was judged, scourged, forced to carry His own cross, and crucified on that hill shaped something like a skull. They call it Golgotha. With the Passover starting at sundown, they had to work hard to get the crosses up, in order that the two thieves and Jesus might die beforehand. It was the law. When He had died, He was buried and the crypt sealed, with a guard placed around it.

The real story happened after the Passover, however, for when the women went to the grave to prepare His body for burial they were at once amazed to discover the stone rolled away and the tomb empty. Angels of God told them that Jesus had risen from the grave. The word, He "lives" spread like wildfire throughout the city.

The disciples, still in shock and deep mourning, were closeted behind locked doors in the upper room. They couldn't believe what had happened, and some of them ran to the tomb to see for themselves.

Mary Magdalene saw the Lord in the cemetery garden. She didn't recognize Him either when first He came. She thought He was the gardener, but when He spoke her name, she knew it was the risen Christ.

But she was not the only one who did not recognize Jesus. I didn't either, neither did my companion as we walked along the highway leading to Emmaus. Perhaps it was the strain of death, the crucifixion, that changed His appearance, but I think not. I think rather it was because the heavenly Father had given Him victory that He looked so different. The burden had been removed. His face shone. His eyes were not sad any longer . . . they burned with the flame of triumph.

He walked with us to Emmaus. He asked my friend and me (so deep in discussion over what had happened were we that we had not even greeted our fellow traveler), "What is this conversation which you are holding with each other as you walk?"

I could not believe He hadn't heard the story of Jesus' resurrection. "Are you the only visitor to Jerusalem who does not know the things that have happened there in these days?" I asked.

And when He replied, "What things?" I was dumbfounded. I answered, "Concerning Jesus of Nazareth, who was a prophet mighty in deed and word before God and all the people, and how our chief priests and rulers delivered Him up to be condemned to death, and crucified Him." "We had hoped," I said sadly, "that He was the one to redeem Israel. Yes, and besides all this it is now the third day since this happened. Moreover, some women of our company amazed us. They were at the tomb early in the morning and did not find His body; and they came back saying that they have even seen a vision of angels, who said that He was alive. Some of those who were with us went to the tomb, and found it just as the women had said; but Him they did not see."

It was so strange . . . wonderful, yet hard to believe. I'm from Emmaus, you know, and I must be shown.

It was then the stranger's eyes . . . beautiful, warm . . . flashed with a look I had seen before. He said, "How dull you are! . . . How slow to believe all that the prophets said! Was the Messiah not bound to suffer thus before entering upon His glory?' Then he began with Moses and all the prophets and explained to us the passages which referred to Himself in every part of the Scriptures.

We were captured by His words. He spoke with such magnificent authority. It was not long until we had reached Emmaus . . . it was only 6 or 7 miles from Jerusalem. He seemed to be going further, but we begged Him to stay with us and tell us more. It was when we sat down to eat in my companion's home that it all became clear as the water of the mountain streams.

He took bread and said the blessing; He broke the bread and offered it to us, and then we saw our unknown stranger was Jesus. And He vanished from our sight.

We were so amazed, yet my friend said, "Did we not feel our hearts on fire as He talked with us on the road and explained the Scriptures to us?"

We were nobodies until then. When He walked into our lives as the risen Lord we became somebody . . . somebody about whom He was concerned . . . somebody for whom He died . . . somebody who needed His love . . . somebody! It was that one event that put my name into Holy Scripture. Your name will never appear in the Bible, but it may appear in God's Book of Life if you, like my traveling companion and I, meet the Savior, listen to Him and receive Him into your heart as we did into our home. He will transform you from a nobody into a somebody, who will always be a somebody in His eyes.

That one event changed the whole pattern of my life. I became not simply a disciple, but an apostle, a preacher. That one brief encounter with the risen Savior has been the fire that has ignited many another soul with the flame of faith. Many disbelieve . . . and in your age there are many who don't believe . . . as in mine. Christians are a minority . . . believing and faithful Christians, that is. The difference between your time and mine is that being a Christian was not taken so lightly then. You not only believed with your mouth, but with your hands and your feet and your mind and heart and soul. To be a Christian could mean death, but death to the Christian is life forever with God.

I wonder how many of you burn with Easter's glow. I wonder how many of you have walked with Jesus, and how many of you walk for Him today into the lives surrounding you with good news that Jesus lives. I wonder if walking with Jesus today will do anything more than change your time schedule one Sunday out of many.

When Jesus interrupted my life, it was an interruption that changed me totally. I had been only a halfhearted disciple. I listened, but I didn't do what He asked. I followed but not in His steps. I served but only when convenient. But now I burst with inner joy for He has risen to make a somebody out of a nobody. He arose to share His triumph with me. And so with you.

I am Cleopas, unknown, but for that one incident in the miracle of Easter. The world may never know your name, but the Lord God does. Recognize Jesus when He comes into your life. Recognize Him, for He comes with salvation for you.

ALLELUIA! CHRIST IS RISEN! HE IS RISEN INDEED!

Quotations: Luke 24:5 NEB; Luke 24:17-24 RSV; Luke 24:25-27, 32 NEB.